REBOOT!

CONFRONTING PTSD ON YOUR TERMS

BY DAVID W. POWELL

Foreword by JOHN DURKIN, PhD

REBOOT! Confronting PTSD on Your Terms: A Workbook
Copyright © 2011 by David W. Powell. All Rights Reserved.
Foreword by John Durkin, PhD

ISBN-13: 978-1-61599-084-9

The authors acknowledge the following people and organizations for allowing us to excerpt their materials:

A Preliminary List of Human Elements reprinted with permission from C. Scott Bolden. For more information please visit http://universallyhumane.wordpress.com

Feelings Inventory from Marshall Rosenberg and the Center for Non-Violent Communication website. http://www.cnvc.org/Training/feelings-inventory

PTSD Worksheet, copyright ©, The Surviving Warrior Project, Inc, 2010 http://www.PTSDhelp.net

Exploring Emotions and Feelings from *Life Skills: Improve the Quality of Your Life with Metapsychology*, copyright © 2005 by Marian K. Volkman

National Center for Post-Traumatic Stress Disorder, www.ncptsd.va

Published by
Loving Healing Press   www.LHPress.com
5145 Pontiac Trail   Tollfree 888-761-6268
Ann Arbor, MI 48105   Fax 734-663-6861

To request a free evaluation copy or purchase multiple copies for a non-profit or service agency at a special discount, please contact us through info@LHPress.com.

Distributed by Ingram Book Group (USA/CAN), Bertram's Books (UK), Hachette Livre (FR), Agapea (SP), Angus & Robertson (AU).

Contents

Foreword

It is an honor to be asked to write this foreword but an honor that is matched by sadness. I was anticipating meeting David for the first time later this year and now realize that his passing has left me with these words as the only opportunity to acknowledge the contribution that he has made, and I expect will continue to make, to the wounded warriors he identified so closely with.

He takes posttraumatic stress disorder (PTSD) and discusses it as a manageable condition, not a medical conundrum. PTSD is a subject held by many in the mental-health community to be so complex as to demand only expert attention, yet David explains it in ways that can be visualized and verbalized by almost anyone. This is how he shows that it is within our own capabilities to do much of the work that can lead to resolution and personal growth. Such self-reliance and insight allows areas of experience to be addressed that can be neglected in an entirely expert-led way of thinking about trauma.

David's invitations to explore our bodies for information, examine our needs for lack of fulfillment and appreciate the reality of our emotional lives, all require us to look at ourselves from several perspectives. This has to be done from within, a perspective that no therapist can truly take. Together these perspectives build a framework for progress that will not be found in therapies that seek merely to improve how we feel or distract us from the pain of what we would rather not face.

Drawing on the military obsession with completing inventories David offers a practical way to help us become aware of what we know, and of what we do not know. Inventories work because they inform us not only of what is present, but what is missing. Psychotherapists who witness recovery from trauma will know that the spark that triggers positive change is often found in what the distressed did not, could not, or dare not, speak of. So David invites us to look where we would rather not look, with a conviction that leaves us in little doubt that because he did it and changed for the better, he believes we all can. He offers hope yet instills confidence. He offers opinion yet expresses authority. He speaks in a way that assures us that he knows that positive change awaits all who are willing to do the work, regardless of the history that keeps us from fully living our lives.

This book, like a good friend, is collaborative, supportive and tolerant, qualities that combat veterans like David knew were vital to their own well-being and their trust in each other. But as veterans with PTSD also know, survival can be problematic. They were warriors, a distinct minority of people whose respect for life and justice got tested in ways that few other people are ever tested.

David's passing also serves as a reminder of life's uncertainty and the fragility of the assumption that tomorrow will arrive for us to complete our work. David has completed his and I hope was proud of this, the final book that he wrote. It has been written by a friend, a friend I did not meet in person, but one I met in spirit through the affection and encouragement that permeates his work. David Powell was a warrior who found peace and a friend who wrote this workbook to help us to see where we might find it too.

John Durkin, PhD

Introduction

Reboot the machine! Stop! Time out! Hold the presses! Back up and regroup! Don't take another step forward! Whoa! Don't just turn off the machine; unplug it from the wall!

I'm just trying to get your attention, friend. (Smile!)

I know that attempting to get control over the life-changing traumas you have endured calls for your immediate action. I want to help you prepare to meet that challenge with all the strength you'll need to do the "work" that lies ahead of you. I'm very familiar with that work, because I've been there. I've done that.

Here's a brief sketch of the events leading up to my Post Traumatic Stress Disorder (PTSD) experience. I'm a former U.S. Marine. I served in the Infantry, fighting in Viet Nam from October 1966 through November 1967. I participated in at least 12 major battles and hundreds of squad, platoon, and company-size operations against the enemy. I was shot and received the Purple Heart. I was exposed to a number of traumatic events that eventually damaged me enough to warrant a 100% disability rating by the Veterans Administration.

My personal quest for therapeutic help has taken me through several methodologies. My therapeutic experiences have taught me that there are good and not so good techniques out there. I'll be talking about my "recipe" for success later. I now have enough self-respect and self-confidence to fully engage in life as I know it, and I believe my suggestions for success will help you too.

Since PTSD is among the least responsive to *self-help* of all the emotional disturbances, I strongly encourage you to find a professional therapist who can work with you on your problems. In this booklet, you'll find brief descriptions of the most popular mental health treatment programs that are available. My aim is to sow the seeds of hope for you, not to suggest that you can do it on your own. In a nutshell, your condition cannot be effectively resolved without professional guidance.

I'm not trying to bash any therapy or therapist here. Instead, I'll be offering situations and themes for you to look at, analyze, and choose to go forward with or cast aside as you continue on your path toward health and recovery. My opinions are mine, and I'm strongly motivated to share them with you.

Think about this. If you were going to build a house, you wouldn't start by making the roof, would you? No, probably not.

When planning to build a house you probably would examine the ground you intend to build on, then check out the materials you'd need, determine the steps you'd take as the construction proceeded, set the phases and dates of completion you'd strive for, and set a target date when you'd have the house finished.

Just as a house needs to be built *up* from its foundation, likewise, one's mental health needs to be rebuilt, *up* from *its* foundation. Many therapists (mainly and unwisely) address *current* PTSD symptoms (the roof) without ever effectively resolving the *earlier* underlying trauma (the foundation) that the PTSD rests on.

I believe that little (or no) attention is placed on the *physical condition* of the client. Also, the psychological *needs* are seldom (if ever) reviewed. I think it's wrong to begin working on PTSD traumas before the physical and emotional foundations of the client are examined, and appropriate corrective measures are taken before PTSD work is started.

Many therapists may be extremely reluctant to say anything to a client that would trigger a traumatic reaction. In some cases, they may fail to consider referring their PTSD clients to someone who *is* trained to deal with that sort of thing.

As with my homebuilding example, why not take the time to set up some alternative priorities as you seek recovery from your horrendous experiences? When you're ready to work on your traumatic incidents, know that only *you* know what *you* are and are not willing and able to confront in therapy at any given time. It's your call.

I know I'm treading on thin ice when I ask you to put your fears aside and have a deep, honest look at what you went through. I wouldn't ask you to do it if I didn't believe with all my heart that you'll make it through to the other side. Remember, mere words can't harm you, unless you don't use them to tell what happened. You have the strength and courage to face and defeat your dragons. Now is as good a time as any to take on those dragons.

You choose if and when you want to dive directly into your "baggage." You're in the wrong office if the therapist has taken it upon himself to judge, unilaterally, what *he* needs to dive into and when to do it. I'd also like to point out that it isn't wise to dive into traumatic memories with a therapist who isn't prepared (by reason of training, experience and available time) to resolve the target incident in the same session. Many therapists, even some trauma specialists unfortunately, bite off more than they can chew at one sitting.

Many PTSD clients are, in fact, quite ready to take that dive when they first show up for therapy. Others are not at all ready and won't be for weeks. The well trained trauma therapist will not treat both of these cases the same. Instead, he will take his cue regarding a client's readiness for a given procedure from the client himself.

Let's look at a small part of the "bible" of the American Psychiatric Association, the Diagnostic and Statistical Manual (DSM). I've pulled some of the language out of the PTSD section and put it here. It's so impersonal, I get chills reading it. Don't be fooled by what you hear. PTSD is *not* a medical condition. And, hold my feet to the fire... with the right therapeutic approach, it is completely reversible!

Diagnostic criteria for 309.81 Posttraumatic Stress Disorder

A. The person has been exposed to a traumatic event in which both of the following were present:

1. The person experienced, witnessed, or was confronted with an event or events that involved actual or threatened death or serious injury, or a threat to the physical integrity of self or others.

2. The person's response involved intense fear, helplessness, or horror.

B. The traumatic event is persistently re-experienced in one (or more) of the following ways:

1. Recurrent and intrusive distressing recollections of the event, including images, thoughts, or perceptions.

2. Recurrent distressing dreams of the event.

3. Acting or feeling as if the traumatic event were recurring (includes a sense of reliving the experience, illusions, hallucinations, and dissociative flashback episodes, including those that occur on awakening or when intoxicated[1]).

4. Intense psychological distress at exposure to internal or external cues that symbolize or resemble an aspect of the traumatic event.

5. Physiological reactivity on exposure to internal or external cues that symbolize or resemble an aspect of the traumatic event.

---

[1] Learn the clinical terms at
http://www.behavenet.com/capsules/disorders/intoxication.htm

What's Your Experience?

If you are currently under the care of a mental health clinician, please answer the following questions:

- Does the individual you are working with seem ambivalent about your current condition and future improvement?
- Are you tense (wired up) before your sessions begin?
- Do you leave the sessions feeling like you are re-experiencing a traumatic event?
- Do you feel like you are "teaching" the counselor about PTSD?
- Do you feel like you are getting nowhere?
- Do you feel like quitting, but are concerned what your relatives and/or close friends will think about your stopping treatment, and think of you as a "quitter"?

"Yes," "No" and "I don't know" answers are all correct. It's OK not to "know." I'm not trying to convince you to "stay the course" nor to abandon it. I'm only trying to give you an opportunity to realistically evaluate the care you may or may not be getting.

In early 1986, at a Vet Center close to where I lived at the time (the Bay Area near San Francisco, California), I had a one-time meeting with a mental health clinician for a problem I had with a personal relationship. Specifically, I didn't trust my live-in girlfriend. Also, I was strongly resistant to letting others get to know me on a personal level, due in no small part to the near-constant PTSD re-experiencing I was trying to deal with and keep hidden on a daily basis.

When our meeting concluded, the clinician invited me to join a start-up therapy group. "It'll be made up of Combat-experienced veterans. The group will meet Thursday nights at the Menlo Park, (California) Veterans Administration campus." (The Menlo Park campus at that time was thought of as "Mecca" for PTSD treatment.)

I accepted the clinician's invitation and began my journey to seek help and recovery. I didn't know much about PTSD back then, and I rejected the notion that I might be suffering from the effects of *any* mental illness, but I was willing to try anything to improve my life.

A Survey of Therapeutic Approaches

Before we embark on *your* journey toward recovery, I want to lightly touch on some of the most popular therapeutic approaches to the treatment of PTSD as we know them today. I have chosen not to go into much detail about any of them. You may find one or more of these approaches valuable to you.[2]

Group therapy / Support Group This is practiced in VA PTSD Clinics and Vet Centers for military veterans and in mental health and crisis clinics, for victims of assault and abuse. A group of *peers* provides a therapeutic setting, because trauma survivors are able to risk sharing traumatic material with the safety, cohesion, and empathy provided by other survivors. It is easier to accept confrontation from a fellow sufferer who has like credentials as a trauma survivor than from a professional therapist who never went through those experiences first-hand.

A PTSD support group is not intended to resolve or cure its members' PTSD. Its purpose is simply to help them acquire more effective ways of living and coping with its intrusive symptoms. Because they mainly regard their target disorders as "incurable," support groups of all sorts tend to run on indefinitely over time. The best known such support group is AA.

Exposure Therapy involves therapeutically confronting a past trauma by repeatedly imagining it in great detail, intended to help the patient face and gradually defuse the fear and distress that was overwhelming in the trauma, and must be done very carefully in order not to re-traumatize the patient.

Done properly and thoroughly, an exposure therapy "worth its salt" should leave the patient with no remaining trauma-related fear or other overwhelming emotion to control. It also should put an end to the patient's vulnerability to being triggered and re-traumatized by subsequent recall of and thinking or talking about the trauma. This is the reasonable expectation one can have of the exposure therapy called Traumatic Incident Reduction, the last procedure on this list.

Eye Movement Desensitization and Reprocessing (EMDR). A therapist guides the client in vividly but safely recalling distressing past experiences ("desensitization") and gaining new understanding "reprocessing") of the events, the bodily and emotional feelings, and the thoughts and self-images associated with them. The "eye movement" aspect of EMDR involves the client moving his/her eyes in a back-and-forth ("saccadic") manner while recalling the event(s).

Cognitive Behavior (CB). I've taken the liberty of grouping together the next three entries on this list of therapeutic approaches, because there's too little

---

[2] Learn more at www.ptsdsupport.net

difference between them to justify a separate listing for each. I've bullet indented them to call attention to their regrouping.

There are a dozen or so different styles of cognitive-behavioral intervention, most of them identified with their key developers (e.g., Ellis, Maultsby, Meichenbaum, Beck and others). The only one represented here by name is Albert Ellis' Rational Emotive Behavior Therapy (REBT). The basic principles articulated in the relevant paragraphs below, are common to all CB styles, which is why they could reasonably be collapsed into just one entry.

- **Cognitive-restructuring therapy** involves learning skills for coping with anxiety and negative thoughts. Cognitive restructuring, also known as cognitive reframing can help people identify, challenge and alter stress-inducing thought patterns and beliefs. The end goal of cognitive restructuring is to replace stress-inducing thoughts with more accurate and less rigid thinking habits.

  Exposing a person to their fears or prior traumas without having them first learning coping techniques—such as relaxation or imagery exercises—can result in their simply being re-traumatized by the event or fear. Therefore, most therapy is conducted within a psychotherapeutic relationship with a therapist trained and experienced with the technique and the related coping exercises.

- **Cognitive-behavioral therapy** is based on the idea that our *thoughts* cause our feelings and behaviors, not external things, like people, situations, and events. The benefit of this is that we can change the way we *think* in order to be able to *feel* and/or *act* better, even though the situation does not change.

- **Rational Emotive Behavior Therapy (REBT).** The main purpose of REBT is to help clients to replace absolute philosophies, full of "musts" and "shoulds" with more realistic and flexible ones; part of this includes learning to accept that all human beings (including themselves) are fallible, and learning to increase their tolerance for frustration while trying to achieve their goals. It holds to the same 'core conditions' as person-centered counseling—empathy, unconditional positive regard, and counselor genuineness—in the counseling relationship. REBT views these conditions as *neither necessary nor sufficient* for therapeutic change to occur. I believe both of these items are important.

Virtual Reality Exposure Therapy (VRET). Patients undergoing this therapy explain to the therapist what happened that caused the trauma, and are exposed to a variety of computer-generated stimuli. The therapy is designed to promote a multi-sensory emotional connection to the memory, helping the patient be able to gradually face the traumatic experiences that underlie his or her distressing memories.

Psychodynamic Psychotherapy focuses on the emotional conflicts caused by the traumatic event. Through the retelling of the traumatic event to a calm, empathic, compassionate and non-judgmental therapist, the patient achieves a greater sense of self-esteem, develops effective ways of thinking and coping, and more successfully deals with the intense emotions that emerge during therapy.

Emotional Freedom Techniques (EFT) differ from conventional psychology. They contend that the cause of all negative emotions is a disruption in the body's energy system. EFT attempts to relieve symptoms by utilizing a routine of gently tapping with the fingertips on a series of points on the body that correspond to acupuncture points on the energy meridians. Where there is an imbalance, there is a corresponding blockage in the flow of energy through the meridian system. The tapping serves to release the blockages that are created when a person thinks about or becomes involved in an emotionally disturbing circumstance. To the degree that the client thinks about the situation which led up to the emotion, EFT can be said to be exposure based.

Traumatic Incident Reduction (TIR) is a systematic method of locating, reviewing and resolving traumatic events. Once a person has used TIR to fully view a painful memory or sequence of related memories, life events no longer trigger the trauma and cause distressing symptoms. TIR is useful in relieving a wide range of fears, limiting beliefs, suffering due to losses (including unresolved grief and mourning), depression, and other symptoms of trauma.

We've had a general look at the landscape now and, hopefully, you're ready to prepare yourself for your walk back home, to that place you once knew. Yes, PTSD changed you. But with the right kind of help, you'll find that *you are still you,* and at that point, with an unburdened heart.

We'll take some inventories of your human anatomy, and next do a *needs* inventory, and some fairly detailed PTSD inventories (not just for combat-traumatized sufferers, but for *all sufferers*). Then we'll examine the basic *emotions,* explore some *needs* and *feelings,* and take a second look at the trauma rehab methodologies.

Section 1 – Inventories

A major influence on my thinking about getting a handle on my PTSD came from the writings of Abraham H. Maslow. Way back in the early 1940s, he put forth his concept of a "Hierarchy of Needs" that he believed applied to all mankind. Below is his pyramid[3].

Maslow's Hierarchy of Needs

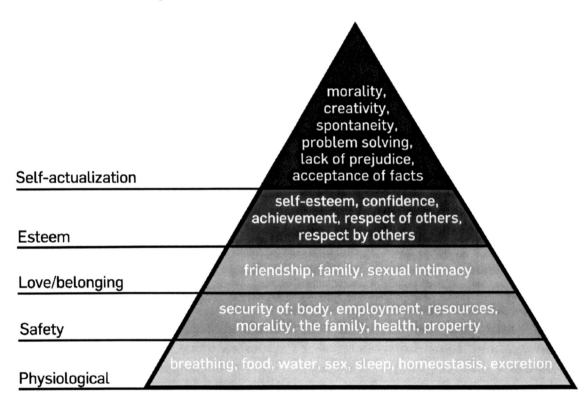

His peers went on to explain this theory, in summary, as the following:

- Maslow's hierarchy of needs is constructed in a specific order. It is depicted as a pyramid consisting of five levels.
- The lowest level is associated with physiological needs.

---

[3] http://psychology.about.com/od/theoriesofpersonality/a/hierarchyneeds.htm

- The higher needs only come into focus when the lower needs are met.
- Once an individual has moved upward to the next level, needs in the lower level will no longer be prioritized.
- If a lower set of needs is no longer being met, the individual will temporarily focus his/her attention on the unfulfilled needs, but will not permanently slip back to the lower level.
- The uppermost level is associated with self-actualization needs, particularly those related to identity and purpose.

For instance, a businessman at the Esteem level who is diagnosed with cancer will spend a great deal of time concentrating on his health (physiological needs), but will continue to value his work performance (esteem needs) and will likely return to work during periods of remission.

I liked the idea of having an order of needs and a sequence of them, one following another until one pyramid level was completed and then moving up to the next one.

Biological Needs Assessment

However, I took his ideas and stretched them backward, finding *biological* needs that I felt should be looked at and worked on before I got into the *psychological* aspects of repairing myself. Here are the steps:

- Get yourself a notebook with a lot of blank sheets. You'll be making notes for later reference as we go along.
- Look at (or imagine) your skeleton, from the tips of your toes, up to the tips of your fingers, up to the top of your head, and every bone in between.
- Are they all there? If any of them are broken, can they be repaired by a doctor? If any of them are missing, can they be replaced with artificial limbs? Are the broken or missing bones necessary for you to live a reasonably normal life?
- If you need to work on or repair your skeleton, write down what needs attention in your notebook.
- Look at (or imagine) your muscles and skin, again from tip to tip.
- If you have to repair or replace injured or missing flesh, write it down.
- Look at (or imagine) your internal organs, each of them independently.
- If you have to repair or replace injured or missing organs, write it down.
- Look at (or imagine) your body chemistry, mainly blood, breathing, and hormones.

- If you have to correct your body chemistry, write it down.

NOTE: Don't put off health care needs. If you have been functioning in an OK manner until now, maybe you can discuss them with your health care provider after you've finished the work I encourage you to do here.

I know that you probably skimmed over the preceding questions and put off the writing work. Please don't take these exercises too lightly.

Think of your body as a *vehicle*. This is the only transportation you'll have to take you from your psychological pain to the sanctuary of life in the present-time world. You want to be assured that it can transport you from start to finish without worrying that it may break down between here and there.

Now we can take a look at your emotional experiences. We'll do that with inventory-like questions. Just be completely honest and non-judgmental with yourself when you read and answer the questions.

Section 2 – Taking Your *Needs* Inventory

NOTE: Make copies of the pages that I ask you to mark on. You'll be referring to these sheets from time to time for many months. If you mark the book pages, you won't have clean sheets to record any new information.

Now we have a handle on the condition of our *physical* body. Let's have a look at your *psychological*. We'll be doing these inventories in preparation for the PTSD work later on.

In order to humanely survive and thrive, people should experience satisfaction that their basic *needs* have been met. Ask yourself if each of these statements is currently and personally true for you without passing any judgment on yourself.

Place a checkmark to the left of the statement if you believe it's TRUE for you, otherwise leave the line unchanged.

Has your *need* been satisfied?

_____ to have good health

_____ for shelter

_____ for clean water

_____ to breathe clean air

_____ for healthy food

_____ for access to consistent and sustainable sources of energy

_____ to exercise caution in uncertain times/places

_____ to believe (have "faith")

_____ to rationalize

_____ to dream

_____ to seek, define and understand your own identity

_____ to be free

_____ to have the opportunity to follow and act on your own will

_____ to be self-determinate

_____ to *not* be dominated

_____ to dominate or manipulate a situation, scenario or person

_____ to be aggressive

_____ to be passive

_____ to be complacent

_____ to understand and seek truth

_____ to be curious

_____ to be mischievous

_____ to be "good"

_____ to be "bad"

_____ to be expressive, physically, intellectually and emotionally

_____ to receive expressions of love, admiration, and/or affection

_____ to outwardly express love, admiration or affection

_____ to destroy

_____ to create

_____ to procreate

_____ to accomplish and move on to the next satisfaction

_____ to feel secure with your emotions, resources, and society (environment)

_____ to enjoy or experience pleasure (in *whatever*)

_____ to be entertained

_____ to be entertaining

_____ to laugh

_____ to cry

_____ to be angry

_____ to be happy

_____ to desire

_____ to grieve

_____ to seek guidance or help: parental, peer, and/or supernatural

_____ for social interaction

_____ for privacy

_____ to share

_____ to covet

_____ to hope for an even better future

_____ to learn through experience and repetition

_____ to apply learned knowledge

_____ to communicate

_____ to leave a legacy

_____ to receive love from yourself

_____ to forgive

_____ to be forgiven

_____ to feel safe

_____ to show respect

_____ to be respected

_____ to contribute to our common humanity

_____ to receive contributions from our common humanity

"Bubbles"

I now take pleasure in introducing you to "Bubbles." It will be a template for many sessions of "color in the bubbles". "Bubbles" is neither male nor female, so the image will work for you regardless of your gender.

NOTE: The only "bubble" you should <u>not</u> color in is the Bubbles' head. No cheating! ...I'll explain why later.

- In keeping with our "home construction" theme, start at the foundation (bottom; feet) of Bubbles, and work your way from left to right, then up a level, and then left to right again.
- For each answer from the *needs* list, if it's checked, color in the bubble. If it's unchecked, do NOT color in the bubble; skip to the next bubble.
- Starting with another Bubbles, for each answer from the *needs* list, if it's NOT checked, color in the bubble. If it's checked, do NOT color in the bubble; skip to the next bubble.

Now you have two physical representations of your *needs*; fulfilled and unfulfilled. Ask yourself this: "With this kind of structure, can I move on to harder psychological work, or do I need to repair this structure before I proceed?"

I recommend you work on your *unfulfilled needs* so you can more aggressively work on your traumas.

If you are the kind of person who likes to have a set of goals you'd like to achieve, then you might want to have a look at your list of *unfulfilled needs* and make them your goals. As you're going over the questions today, I'll bet you'll see where you can pick up "spare time" you can use for more productive purposes.

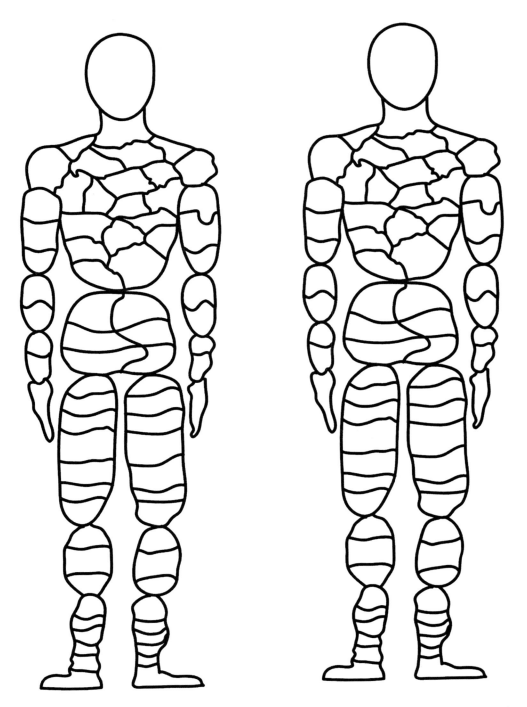

Fill Bubbles #1 with *fulfilled* needs   Fill Bubbles #2 with *unfulfilled* needs

Section 3 – PTSD Inventory for Military Casualties

- If you <u>DO</u> <u>NOT</u> have military-related traumas, you may SKIP this Section.
- If you <u>DO</u>, please continue on.

Digging up the answers to these questions can be difficult. You may (likely will) dig up some painful memories and images. If you get stressed out — take a break. Write down your traumatic events in your notebook. Use a voice recorder if writing isn't your cup of tea.

I've heard some people say you might find a friend to write down your information as you talk. I say *do not do that!* Earlier, I said *peers* provide a therapeutic setting because trauma survivors are able to risk sharing traumatic material with the safety, cohesion, and empathy provided by other survivors[4]. *Friends* usually aren't *peers,* in the sense that they aren't usually trauma survivors.

The following questions are designed to stimulate your recollection of your military experiences. We'll be working on each of your traumatic events in the next Section.

---

[4] More about triggers at http://www.ptsdsupport.net/ptsd_triggers.html

PTSD Worksheet

[Mark your answers in the table following this worksheet]

During your Military Assignment:

1. How often were you on a base?
2. How often were you in the field?

How often did you do the following?

3. Fire a weapon at the enemy
4. Kill or likely kill your target
5. See someone killed or dying
6. Think you'd be killed
7. Think you'd be seriously wounded
8. See dead bodies, civilian or enemy
9. See dead comrades

11. Did you handle any human bodies?
12. Did you participate in firefights?

Did you or your unit experience any of the following?

13. Sniper Fire
14. Rocket/Mortar attacks
15. Personnel Mines/Booby Traps
16. IEDs (targeted at vehicles)
17. Ambush
18. Did you feel that your experiences were overwhelmingly stressful?
19. Did you feel overwhelmed by thirst?
20. Did you feel overwhelmed by hunger?
21. Did you feel overwhelmed by exhaustion?
22. Did you feel there were NO safe places?

Using the table on the next page, mark a box with an "X" (or color in the block) for each answer you gave, selecting the column that matches your answer. Start at the top of each column and work your way down toward the bottom.[5]

---

[5] Derived from *PTSD Worksheet* at http://www.ptsdhelp.net/id18.html

	Never	Rarely	Sometimes	Often	Frequently
1					
2					
3					
4					
5					
6					
7					
8					
9					
10					
11					
12					
13					
14					
15					
16					
17					
18					
19					
20					
21					
22					

Table 3-1: Generic Answer Worksheet

When you have finished filling in the table, you'll see a graphic representation of where you used up some of your "spare time." Although the graphics are interesting, they are past-tense experiences, and should be stored in your long-term memory bank. There isn't a civilian-life, present-time use for them.

Here's an idea: How about setting up another set of goals for yourself? This time you could work on moving the checked items in the 3rd and 4th columns back into the first and second ones. As you're going over the questions today, I'll bet you'll see where you can pick up "spare time" you can use for more productive purposes. Although you can't change your history, you *can* change what you *do* with it.

Section 4 – PTSD Inventory for All Casualties

You've experienced or witnessed life-threatening event(s) that caused you intense fear, helplessness or horror. Of course, the PTSD range of emotions is considerably wider than this, whatever you've experienced is true for *you*.

Digging up the answers to these questions can be difficult. You may (likely will) dig up some painful memories and images. If you get stressed out — take a break. Write down your traumatic events in your notebook. Use a voice or video recorder if writing isn't your cup of tea.

I've heard some people say you might find a friend to write down your information as you talk. I say *do not do that!* Earlier, I said *peers* provide a therapeutic setting because trauma survivors are able to risk sharing traumatic material with the safety, cohesion and empathy provided by other survivors. Likely, your *friends* aren't *peers,* in the sense that they aren't usually trauma survivors.

We're trying to capture your traumatic experiences. For *each event,* write down your answer to the question you are being asked in a brief narrative in enough detail to be able to complete a thorough description of it at a later time.

In a few sentences, write down an overall description of the experience. Examples:

- "We were ambushed while on a patrol in early December 1966."
- "On May 23, 1998, at 8:13 pm, the bastard knocked me out and raped me."

Complete a detailed write-up of each one. Write each one separately, on as much paper as you need.

NOTE: It may help you get through this exercise if you imagine yourself to be a Newspaper Reporter while you are working on this. This way you may remain somewhat unattached to the material and these tasks may be more bearable.

I'm about to ask you some very probing, intimate questions. They'll demand you to use your utmost courage to answer them. Here are a few affirmations I used to get through them:

- "I am alive and can give my answers."
- "It isn't happening again."
- "I can answer them at my own pace; no rush."

- "The answers are my secrets and they can stay that way."
- "The better my answers are, the clearer the experience becomes."
- "I'm the only one who can answer the questions. No one else knows what I went through."

OK, my friend, time to take a deep breath, say a prayer or whatever, and dig in. Here are questions to answer for *each event* you recall.

Ask yourself:
- How you felt immediately before the event
- What you experienced (the event)
- How long did the "pinnacle" last (1 second, a few seconds, a few minutes)
- Who was there, in addition to yourself
- What did you see hear, taste, touch, smell and think
- When did it happen (time of day, day of the week, calendar date, etc.)
- Where were you (geography, surroundings, standing, sitting, etc.)
- Why did the event happen (not just "duty" but your motivations, theirs, etc.)
- What you did during the event
- How you felt about yourself immediately after the event
- How you felt about the others involved after the event
- How you feel about the others involved now

When you have finished the last traumatic event (that you can recall right now), go back and look at each narrative you wrote. Go through the sub-level questions below and provide any details you may have left out the first time through.

When you're finished, answer the following questions.[6]

---

[6] Derived from the *Post-Traumatic Stress Disorder Self-Test*
http://www.ptsd.ne.gov/pdfs/ptsd.pdf

Post-Traumatic Stress Disorder Self-Test

(Circle Best Answer for Each Item)

DO YOU...

1. have repeated, distressing memories and/or dreams of it?

        Never   Rarely   Sometimes   Often   Frequently

2. act or feel like the event is happening again? (Flashbacks)

        Never   Rarely   Sometimes   Often   Frequently

3. feel intense physical and/or emotional pain when you are exposed to things that remind you of it?

        Never   Rarely   Sometimes   Often   Frequently

4. avoid reminders of it?

        Never   Rarely   Sometimes   Often   Frequently

5. avoid thoughts, feelings, or conversations about it?

        Never   Rarely   Sometimes   Often   Frequently

6. avoid activities, places, or people who remind you of it?

        Never   Rarely   Sometimes   Often   Frequently

7. "blank out" on important parts of it?

        Never   Rarely   Sometimes   Often   Frequently

8. avoid things that remind you of the trauma?

        Never   Rarely   Sometimes   Often   Frequently

Since your traumatic experience, do you have...

9. frequent, disturbing memories:

        Never   Rarely   Sometimes   Often   Frequently

10. nightmares:

        Never   Rarely   Sometimes   Often   Frequently

11. flashbacks:

        Never   Rarely   Sometimes   Often   Frequently

12. Has your interest in activities changed since you began experiencing problems related to the trauma?

        Never   Rarely   Sometimes   Often   Frequently

Using a clean "table" (from Section 3), mark a box with an "X" (or color in the block) for each answer you gave, selecting the column that matches your answer. Start at the top of each column and work your way down toward the bottom.

When you have finished filling in the table, you'll see a graphic representation of how your thoughts about your traumas have altered your quality of life, and where you spent some of your "spare time."

Here's an idea: How about setting up another set of goals for yourself? This time you could work on moving the checked items in the third and fourth columns back into the first and second ones.

Now we move to another set of questions about your *traumatized life* in general. DID/DO YOU:

1. lose interest in significant activities of you life?

    Never Rarely Sometimes Often Frequently

2. feel detached from other people?

    Never Rarely Sometimes Often Frequently

3. feel your range of emotions is restricted?

    Never Rarely Sometimes Often Frequently

4. sense that your future has shrunken? (For example, you don't expect to have, or keep a career, marriage, children, or a normal life.)

    Never Rarely Sometimes Often Frequently

5. have problems sleeping?

    Never Rarely Sometimes Often Frequently

6. become irritable or have outbursts of anger?

    Never Rarely Sometimes Often Frequently

7. have problems concentrating?

    Never Rarely Sometimes Often Frequently

8. feel "on guard"?

    Never Rarely Sometimes Often Frequently

9. have an exaggerated "startle response"?

    Never Rarely Sometimes Often Frequently

10. *Have you in the past* intoxicated yourself to cope with the stress of your traumatic experiences?

    Never Rarely Sometimes Often Frequently

11. Do *you now* intoxicate yourself to cope with stress?

    Never Rarely Sometimes Often Frequently

12. Do you ever seem to shut out the world?

    Never Rarely Sometimes Often Frequently

13. Do you feel as if your emotions were drained out of you?

    Never Rarely Sometimes Often Frequently

14. Do you find it hard to control your anger? Specifically, do things that *DIDN'T* bother you before *NOW* do make you angry?

Never   Rarely   Sometimes   Often   Frequently

15. Do you think of suicide or of hurting other people, or both?

Never   Rarely   Sometimes   Often   Frequently

16. Do you feel estranged from others?

Never   Rarely   Sometimes   Often   Frequently

17. Are you uncomfortable in large crowds?

Never   Rarely   Sometimes   Often   Frequently

18. Do you prefer to be alone?

Never   Rarely   Sometimes   Often   Frequently

19. Do loud noises bother you?

Never   Rarely   Sometimes   Often   Frequently

20. Are you jumpy or nervous?

Never   Rarely   Sometimes   Often   Frequently

Using a clean "table" (from Section 3), mark a box with an "X" (or color in the block) for each answer you gave, selecting the column that matches your answer. Start at the top of each column and work your way down toward the bottom.

When you have finished filling in the table, you'll see a graphic representation of how, generally speaking, you look at your present and near-term future.

If you'd like to find "extra time" you need to work on improving your quality of life, consider moving the items checked in the third and fourth columns of the preceding table into the first or second columns.

Section 5 – Exploring Emotions and Feelings

My search for understanding PTSD led me to find some views about how human beings develop their memories, what they're composed of, and what I was missing. I say "missing" because I didn't know why my traumatic events, when triggered, made me feel as though I was *experiencing* them for the *first time*. It wasn't like "Oh, yeah, I remember the time when..." It was more like "I remember that happened, and the next thing I remember is..." See the gap in time?

I decided to look at the category "Emotions" to see if an answer might be there. In my research, I found the following excerpt to be helpful in understanding the scope of human emotions[7].

What is the Emotional Scale?

Whole books could be written about the observed phenomena of the Emotional Scale. The Scale is simply a spectrum of emotions (see Fig. 5-1 on the following page). I am calling it a spectrum rather than just a list of emotions because the theory is that each of the emotions follows or flows into the next, whether one is on the way down, or on the way up the scale. They aren't sharply divided, but rather shade into each other as do the colors of the rainbow. Of course many other emotions could be identified on this spectrum. Figure 5-1 shows the main ones that we tend to work with and talk about all the time.

First of all, let me clarify that there is nothing "wrong" with any of these emotions. They are all appropriate in different circumstances. Two interesting things to study in relation to emotions are:

1. Fixidity or stuckness of a person's emotional level.
2. The appropriateness or inappropriateness of a given emotion in a particular situation.

Of course, the second is a value judgment rather than an objective truth. The fact remains that anyone expressing an emotion that is truly inappropriate to the situation will also probably experience some discomfort along with it. It isn't true that just because an emotion is far down the scale that it is necessarily terribly unpleasant. If someone has done the work to clear out the traumatic aspects of past losses, for example, s/he may experience a new loss as a very pure and in-the-

---

[7] Excerpted from *Life Skills: Improve the Quality of Your Life with Metapsychology* by Marian K. Volkman

present-moment Grief. This is a very different experience from feeling a loss all muddied up with the leftover feelings of sadness from earlier losses.

ELATION
ENTHUSIASM
CHEERFULNESS
CONSERVATISM
COMPLACENCY
CONTENTMENT
AMBIVALENCE
ANTAGONISM
ANGER
RESENTMENT
HIDDEN HOSTILITY
ANXIETY
FEAR
GRIEF
APATHY

The Emotional Scale (Fig. 5-1)

After familiarizing yourself with the Emotional Scale, think of some emotions that are not named on the scale. Where would you put them?

Any emotion can have an aesthetic component to it. We can enjoy the beautiful sadness at a tear-jerker movie, or enjoy a delicious thrill of fear in a haunted house. The situations in these examples may be artificial, but the emotions are real.

Another way to look at and understand the Emotional Scale is to consider it as a range of vibration from heavy and slow at the bottom to light and fast at the top. Let's take a look at each of the major emotional levels from the bottom to the top.

Apathy contains a sense of hopelessness, as if the effort to "do something about it" (whatever "it" is), is just too great to contemplate. It is clearly not a very fun emotion, either to be in or to be around, but it can sometimes come with a sort of comfortable numbness, relative to some of the more volatile emotions above it on the scale.

At least a period of temporary Apathy might be expected after a stunning loss such as one's house and possessions being destroyed in a fire or other disaster; the loss of a business one had poured one's life into; or the loss of a long-term life partner. Some of the main factors determining how long that period of Apathy lasts are: the person's own resilience, the support system available, and how much earlier traumatic material got triggered.

Grief covers the gamut from acute frantic despair down to dull sadness, and everything in between. The emotional level of Grief is often accompanied by crying, but a person doesn't have to be crying to be at this level. As a side note, my sister Ellen points out that getting a cold often happens right after a loss of some kind and, "a cold is a slow way of crying." Psycho-neuroimmunology informs us that depression and lower emotions drag the immune system down.

After some period of Apathy in the examples given above, a person may move up into Grief. Again, depending on the circumstances, a person may move through Grief relatively quickly or stay parked there for years. Both Apathy and Grief are heavy, gluey emotions. In this band, a person tends to have most of his/her attention focused inward.

At Fear, a person is starting to look more outward, if only to watch for things that are—or appear to be—sources of threat or danger. Fear may manifest in a person's gaze tending to be frozen, the deer in the headlights phenomenon, or the gaze darting around, scanning the environment for danger.

Though it is up from Apathy and Grief and more active than those lower emotions, Fear is still uncomfortable. Extreme fear is one of the worst emotions to experience. Fear spans the range from griefy, overwhelmed Fear up through a more prickly and outward-facing Fear. Any emotion can vary in volume or intensity as well as the emotional level itself. Fear can vary in intensity from stark terror through a low simmering anxiety.

Hidden Hostility comes between Fear and Anger. The Fear still has enough of a grip that hostility doesn't come out into the open as such, but is veiled. At the same time the person's reach is extending outward more now. Everyone hurts others inadvertently at times. However, someone at the level of Hidden Hostility makes a habit of saying and doing hurtful things while pretending friendship or at the least, indifference. The psychological term for this is "passive-aggressive behavior."

At Resentment, hostility is now out in the open, though it is seething and simmering rather than lashing out. At this point, a person has moved up out of the long shadow of Apathy and is starting to feel that although the current situation is unfavorable, something might be (and should be!) done about it.

Not yet fully owning his or her personal power and responsibility, someone at Resentment is starting to cause bigger effects on the environment, though this person would prefer that the work be done by someone else.

Anger has the strongest outward focus so far. It comes in either hot or cold mode. This emotion can be a powerful force for getting things done; at the same time it can be very harsh and abrasive if directed either at self or other people. Anger can be a positive force if it is directed at appropriate situations and properly focused. It has a very bad name with many people, because of its getting mixed up destructiveness.

Antagonism brings in a lighter note of playfulness for the first time as we move up the scale. Here a person is looking for change (usually in the object of his/her antagonism) but without the heaviness of Resentment. Since it is lighter, less serious, and more bantering, relationships based in Antagonism can look wildly successful compared to relationships between people much farther down the scale. Fiction, especially in TV and film, portray this sort of relationship often between the leading characters, whether they be couples, friends or people who work together. Trading witty quips, though not the pinnacle of intimacy, makes for lively entertainment and from some vantage points on the emotional scale may look to be as good as it gets.

At Ambivalence, a person has achieved a sort of autonomy. In fact in the whole band of Ambivalence – Contentment – Complacency we see a new tolerance for situations and other people. At Ambivalence, a person is still looking for something outside of him or her to come along and provide some interest and entertainment. This person has a very "take it or leave it" attitude toward life.

At Contentment, a person does not have a big drive to get things done, but is a master at enjoying what is. A person in Contentment is generally very pleasant to be around.

At Complacency, a person is more actively pleased in what s/he has wrought in the world. At Contentment and Complacency, a person has got life about where s/he wants it to be and interested in conserving and maintaining this achievement.

Cheerfulness is a new plateau of engagement and activity, as a person at this level is very willing to reach out and involve others in his or her schemes.

Enthusiasm brings another level of intensity to the person's degree of causativeness. Where we saw a person at Ambivalence looking about (even if languidly) for something interesting to come along, at Cheerfulness and Enthusiasm s/he is looking around for new games to start. Explorers, inventors, and entrepreneurs are often (though certainly not always) in the cheerful-enthusiastic band.

Elation is a peak state emotion. We aren't talking here about some sort of giddy glee, but rather that profound sense of connectedness with life that is usually remembered and treasured long after the event of experiencing it. At Elation, life is satisfying and exquisite, full of possibility and promise.

~~~

After studying the Emotional Scale, my self-talk and communication with others became much easier. Before I learned about emotions, I found that when I tried to describe how I *felt*, I was choosing words from a long list of feelings, but now I look at the much shorter *emotions* list and can give a more concise answer.

The following list may help you set more goals for yourself. As you identify your negative feelings, consider making it a goal to rid yourself of them.

Feelings When Your Needs Are Not Satisfied

Fear	Aversion	Disquiet	Pain	Tension
apprehensive	animosity	agitated	agony	anxious
dread	appalled	alarmed	anguished	cranky
foreboding	contempt	disconcerted	bereaved	distressed
frightened	disgusted	disturbed	devastated	distraught
mistrustful	dislike	perturbed	grief	edgy
panicked	hate	rattled	heartbroken	fidgety
petrified	horrified	restless	hurt	frazzled
scared	hostile	shocked	lonely	irritable
suspicious	repulsed	startled	miserable	jittery nervous
terrified		surprised	regretful	overwhelmed
wary	**Confused**	troubled	remorseful	restless
worried	ambivalent	turbulent		stressed out
	baffled	turmoil	**Sad**	
Annoyed	bewildered	uncomfortable	depressed	**Vulnerable**
aggravated	dazed	uneasy	dejected	fragile
dismayed	hesitant	unnerved	despair	guarded
disgruntled	lost	unsettled	despondent	helpless
displeased	mystified	upset	disappointed	insecure
exasperated	perplexed		discouraged	leery
frustrated	puzzled	**Embarrassed**	disheartened	reserved
impatient	torn	ashamed	forlorn	sensitive
irritated		chagrined	gloomy	shaky
irked	**Disconnected**	flustered	heavy hearted	
	alienated	guilty	hopeless	**Yearning**
Angry	aloof	mortified	melancholy	envious
enraged	apathetic	self-conscious	unhappy	jealous
furious	bored		wretched	longing
incensed	cold	**Fatigue**		nostalgic
indignant	detached	beat		pining
irate	distant	burnt out		wistful
livid	distracted	depleted		
outraged	indifferent	exhausted		
resentful	numb	lethargic		
	removed	listless		
	uninterested	sleepy		
	withdrawn	tired		
		weary		
		worn out		

The following list may help you set more goals for yourself. As you identify your positive feelings, consider adding the ones you don't currently have to the ones you do have.

Feelings When Your Needs Are Satisfied

Affectionate	Confident	Grateful	Peaceful
compassionate	empowered	appreciative	calm
friendly	open	moved	clear headed
loving	proud	thankful	comfortable
open hearted	safe	touched	centered
sympathetic	secure		content
tender		**Inspired**	equanimous
warm	**Exhilarated**	amazed	fulfilled
	blissful	awed	mellow
Engaged	ecstatic	wonder	quiet
absorbed	elated		relaxed
alert	enthralled	**Joyful**	relieved
curious	exuberant	amused	satisfied
engrossed	radiant	delighted	serene
enchanted	rapturous	glad	still
entranced	thrilled	happy	tranquil
fascinated		jubilant	trusting
interested	**Excited**	pleased	
intrigued	amazed	tickled	**Refreshed**
involved	animated		enlivened
spellbound	ardent		rejuvenated
stimulated	aroused		renewed
	astonished		rested
Hopeful	dazzled		restored
expectant	eager		revived
encouraged	energetic		
optimistic	enthusiastic		
	giddy		
	invigorated		
	lively		
	passionate		
	surprised		
	vibrant		

Section 6 – Memory and Trauma

Dissociation: a splitting in awareness; memory loss.

Dissociation[8], described by those with PTSD, include an altered sense of time, reduced sensations of pain, and the presence or absence of terror or horror—resembling the observations of those who have responded by freezing during a traumatic threat. It appears that the greatest pains of PTSD result from dissociation. While dissociation is an instinctive response to save the self from suffering, it also exacts a high price in return.

In my opinion, working on your dissociation is *not* like you will be opening Pandora's Box. Pandora's "box" was actually a jar, a large jar given to Pandora and contained all the evils of the world. Opening Pandora's box released those evils and that release couldn't ever be undone. This won't be the case when you *Confront Your PTSD.*

Pieces of the event that are not consiously remembered make the would-be memory fragmented and incomplete. The resulting recollection is like a string of beads, with the threading string broken in one or more places.

Unless and *until* a traumatic experience can be fully processed in the mind (experienced in its entirety, start to end), it will remain an "incomplete" event and will be at risk of being triggered again and again.

The consequences of trauma and PTSD vary greatly. In general, victims of PTSD suffer with a reduced quality of life due to the intrusive symptoms. There may be periods of over-activity or periods of exhaustion as their bodies suffer the effects of hyper-arousal.

Reminders of the trauma they suffered may appear suddenly, causing panic, and possible flashbacks. They become fearful, not only of the trauma itself, but of their own reactions to the trauma. Body signals that were at one time "safe" become dangerous.

When reminders of trauma become extreme, freezing or dissociation can be activated, just as if the trauma were occurring in the present. Victims of PTSD can become extremely restricted, fearing to be together with others or to go out of their homes.

---

[8] For more information, see http://en.wikipedia.org/wiki/Dissociation

Traumatic memories are processed differently from ordinary memories. During a traumatic experience, our brain fires off signals that tell our body it's time for "fight, flee or freeze." Our brain can experience an overload. The result is our inability to organize the traumatic event into a coherent, verbally represented narrative.

Sexual assault, especially when it occurs during childhood, might result in repressed memories of the event. Case studies tell the story of many victims who "forgot" all or part of the details about their assault, even in cases where there was evidence of the crimes, such as medical evaluations, testimony from other victims and even confessions from the perpetrator. Memories of sexual assault are more likely to be repressed if the victim was very young at the time, or if the crime was particularly violent.

People who have experienced other traumatic events, such as car accidents, combat, or even life in the inner city, where they might frequently witness acts of violence, can also experience memory loss.

That's a long-winded way of explaining why re-experiencing a traumatic event happens. The memories associated with the event are incomplete, so the emotional charge associated with them, although generally suppressed, remains potentially intrusive until the experience can be more fully understood (through a properly guided professional intervention). Once the memory is unsuppressed and viewed in its totality, the charge dissipates, and the experience takes its place alongside other benign long-term memories.

Rather than go into each of the therapies in more detail I listed in Section 1 in more detail, it's enough for me to say that I was unsuccessful with the ones I tried, until I found TIR.

Group therapy (Support Group): A group of *peers* provides this therapeutic setting. Support groups of all sorts tend to run on indefinitely over time. The best known such support group is AA.

Mistakenly, I thought this structure would work well for me. It didn't because there was no *peer* who had experienced my traumas *exactly like me.*

Exposure Therapy: Exposure in this context means confronting a past trauma by recalling and reviewing it in great detail. You may see the word "imaginal" used in describing Exposure Therapy because you re-imagine the scene. I wanted to have this be a part of my overall treatment. I found it in the exposure therapy called Traumatic Incident Reduction, the last procedure on this list.

Eye Movement Desensitization and Reprocessing (EMDR): The "eye movement" aspect of EMDR involves the client moving his/her eyes in a back-and-forth ("saccadic") manner while recalling the event(s).

I didn't look into this method. I felt I was already distracted enough, and was put off by the "darting eyes" requirement.

Cognitive-Behavioral Therapy (CBT): The goal of these nearly identical procedures is to replace stress-inducing thoughts with more accurate and less rigid thinking habits.

Most therapy is conducted within a psychotherapeutic relationship with a therapist trained and experienced with the technique and the related coping exercises. CBT and Rational Emotive Behavior Therapy (REBT) are based on the concept "Our *thoughts* cause our feelings and behaviors, not external things, like people, situations and events."

I applied this concept to my generalized traumatic thinking. (See the last set of questions in Section 3). Also, I find this a useful tool for reprocessing negative conclusions in the here-and-now.

Virtual Reality Exposure Therapy (VRET): The therapy is designed to promote a multi-sensory emotional connection to the memory.

I didn't try this method either. I felt I was already distracted enough, and didn't need to experience an artificial reality on top of it.

Psychodynamic Psychotherapy: Through the retelling of the traumatic event to a calm, empathic, compassionate and non-judgmental therapist, the patient achieves a greater sense of self-esteem, develops effective ways of thinking and coping, and more successfully deals with the intense emotions that emerge during therapy.

Emotional Freedom Techniques (EFT): Attempts to relieve symptoms by utilizing a routine of tapping with the fingertips on a series of points on the body that correspond to acupuncture points on the energy meridians.

They start with statements that begin, for example: "Even though I have this memory..." or "Even though I committed this act..." and complete this statement with the phrase: "I deeply and completely accept myself."

I personally incorporate this acceptance phrase whenever I reflect upon past deeds that I deem "out of the "envelope" of ordinary human experience. However, the tapping is the main practice which distinguishes EFT.

Traumatic Incident Reduction (TIR): Can relieve a wide range of fears, limiting beliefs, suffering due to losses (including unresolved grief and mourning), depression, and other traumatic symptoms. Read on to Section 7 for details.

Section 7 – Why I Chose Traumatic Incident Reduction (TIR)

I was impressed with the professionalism of the TIR people and their respect for the privacy of information disclosed during my sessions. Of course, this was in marked contrast to how I felt in Group Therapy. The statements that follow were expressed to me before I started my TIR sessions:

Before we begin *any* session, here are a few rules we follow:

- Without your express permission, no recordings of any kind are taken of *any* session.
- Without your express permission, no observers ever watch or listen to *any* session.
- Any and all writings brought to *any* session, or developed by you or me during *any* session, are confidential.

My facilitator (the term that TIR uses in place of "therapist") also made it clear that I needed to be genuinely interested in and focused on doing the work that lay ahead of us. I learned the importance of being prepared to do the kind of work required to be successful. Here are the basic rules I was asked to respect:

- Do not be intoxicated, physically tired, hungry, or thirsty coming into session.
- Be physically well and comfortable coming into session.
- Approve of the lighting, acoustics, temperature, and general ambience of the meeting room.
- Affirm that you are ready to begin the session.

Content and Structure of a TIR Session.

TIR is a brief but thorough, well-ordered and respectful, non-hypnotic, one-on-one procedure for permanently eliminating the negative effects of past traumas. It involves repeated "viewing" of a traumatic memory under conditions designed to enhance safety and minimize distraction. Ignoring the clock, a TIR session always continues until the session agenda is brought to a successful conclusion.

The *client* does most of the work; the facilitator offers *no interpretations* and makes *no judgments*, positive or negative. His/her job is mainly to keep the process on track by giving appropriate instructions to the "viewer" (client). The TIR atmosphere is one of sincere and appropriate acknowledgement, as well as unconditional positive regard.

To begin the procedure, the viewer selects the specific, personally traumatic incident of his or her choice. The incident is then played by the viewer like a videotape. First, it is "rewound" it to the beginning, then viewed as it plays through to the end, without (usually) talking about it while it is being viewed. After the viewer has finished the inner experience of viewing the incident, the facilitator asks what happened, and the viewer can describe the event or his/her inner reactions to going through it.

After the viewer has completed one review (and one description) of the incident, the facilitator guides the viewer through several additional explorations. At no point, though, does the facilitator question, critique or analyze the viewer's experience or remarks. Neither is the viewer ever asked to explain or justify his experience; nor is he ever rushed in any way.

After a few run-throughs, most viewers begin to confront the emotion and uncomfortable details of the incident more thoroughly. Typically, the viewer will reach an emotional peak after several run-throughs, and then, on successive run-throughs, the amount of negative emotion will diminish, until the viewer reaches a point of having no negative emotion about the incident at all.

Instead, the viewer becomes rather thoughtful and contemplative, and usually comes up with one or more insights—often major ones—concerning the trauma, life, or the viewer's own nature. The viewer, often smiles or laughs at this point, but at least manifests calm and serenity. At this point, the viewer has reached an "end point" and the facilitator stops the TIR procedure.

A TIR session is not ended until the viewer reaches such an end point and feels good. This may take anywhere from a few minutes to 3 - 4 hours. The average session time for a new viewer is about 90 minutes. An average of 15 total session hours will eliminate PTSD symptoms for many people in most cases.

Results with TIR

The dissociations embedded in my traumatic experiences were now clear. My recollections of my traumatic events went from the present-tense "see, hear, taste, touch, smell" to the past-tense "saw, heard, tasted, touched, smelled." In other words, the events became recalled memories, detailed but with no more re-experiencing; they had become ordinary memories. What I had once viewed as "painful recollections" have since become "somber reflections" of what happened so long ago and far away. More like "Yeah—that was sure an interesting experience," rather than my old phrasing, like "Whew—I forget all the details, but I ask myself how I could have done such things?"

In closing, I highly recommend that you find a trained TIR Facilitator, make an appointment for yourself, take along your notebook and the write-ups you've developed as you went through this pamphlet, and see if you feel comfortable working with the Facilitator on your traumatic experiences. You can learn more or get a referral at www.TIR.org.

Epilogue

I did TIR, and I'm a better, happier person now.

Here are a few changes I've made in my life. I won't list them all, but they'll give you some idea of what's possible in *your life* in the not-too-distant future.

I have been intoxicant-free for over two decades. My *air* of self-confidence, a strong handshake, and open conversational style have turned many a "stranger" into an acquaintance or friend. I enjoy a loving one-on-one relationship with Susan. We have been together since 1998. I'm debt-free. Try as they might, even broadcast TV/cable news shows don't get me anywhere near "angry." I have goals that I work on almost daily. My old expectation of a foreshortened life has been amended to "another day done, and the next day will be even more fruitful."

Every 3 to 6 months, I encourage you to go back through this pamphlet, to do the exercises again. I think you'll find that each time you do, you'll see improvement. Then... after your work with TIR has concluded, you may now color in Bubbles' "Head-shaped" bubble. You've earned it (Smile!).

About David W. Powell (1941-2011)

David W. Powell was a native Southern Californian. He was born in East Los Angeles in 1941, and lived in Long Beach, Pasadena, Arcadia, Redondo Beach, and Ventura until his relocation to Northern California in the early 1980s. There, he lived in Sausalito, Foster City, Palo Alto, and Downtown San Francisco. David migrated to Australia in 1974, and then returned to live in Southern California in 1975.

He has been married three times and is the father of four children, Jason, Carissa, Scott, and Thomas.

His vocation was in the computer environment. He was a first, second, and third generation computer programmer, systems analyst, project leader, manager, vice president, executive vice president, and owned his own computer consulting services company.

He graduated from high school and attended several semesters of college courses.

He was a first generation student of Senior Grandmaster Edmund K. Parker, the father of American Kenpo Karate, and attained the rank of Black Belt in 1968.

David lived in Napa, California for over five years before recently relocating to Tucson, Arizona. While there, he penned his memoir *My Tour In Hell: A Marine's Battle with Combat Trauma* (from Modern History Press), a raw and unfiltered expose of living with PTSD for 20 years and his eventual recovery. By sharing his small victories, he hoped to inspire vets everywhere to seek help and never surrender.

In 2007, David was the keynote speaker at the Vermont Veterans Combat Stress Symposium (www.VermontVeterans.com). He appeared on a special episode of "RECON", a series about current military events on *The Pentagon Channel*. He also appeared on *Retirement Living TV* network, as well as numerous talkradio shows, always in service of finding help for veterans and their families.

His was devoted to his mate, Susan, gardening projects at his home in the desert, the study of psychology as it relates to esteem, and what he called superficial explorations into history.

He abhorred war and its aftermath.

David wishes all of us a peaceful, rewarding, happy, fulfilling experience while we are alive, and endeavors to make the lives of others better than they may now be.

You can learn more about David at his site **www.MyTourInHell.com**

For Further Reading

Burtles, J. (2007). *Coping with crisis: A counselor's guide to the restabilization process*. Ann Arbor, MI: Loving Healing Press.

Doherty, G. W. (2007). *Crisis intervention training for disaster workers: An introduction*. Ann Arbor, MI: Rocky Mtn Region Disaster Mental Health Institute.

Gerbode, F. A. (1995). *Beyond psychology: An introduction to metapsychology*. Palo Alto, CA: IRM Press.

Powell, D. W. (2006). *My tour in hell: A Marine's battle with combat trauma*. Ann Arbor, MI: Modern History Press.

Schiraldi, G. R. (2009). *The post-traumatic stress disorder sourcebook: A guide to healing, recovery, and growth*. New York, N.Y.: McGraw-Hill.

Volkman, M. K. (2005). *Life skills: Improve the quality of your life with metapsychology*. Ann Arbor, MI: Loving Healing Press.

Volkman, V. R. (2005). *Beyond trauma: Conversations on traumatic incident reduction*. Ann Arbor, MI: Loving Healing Press.

Extra Forms

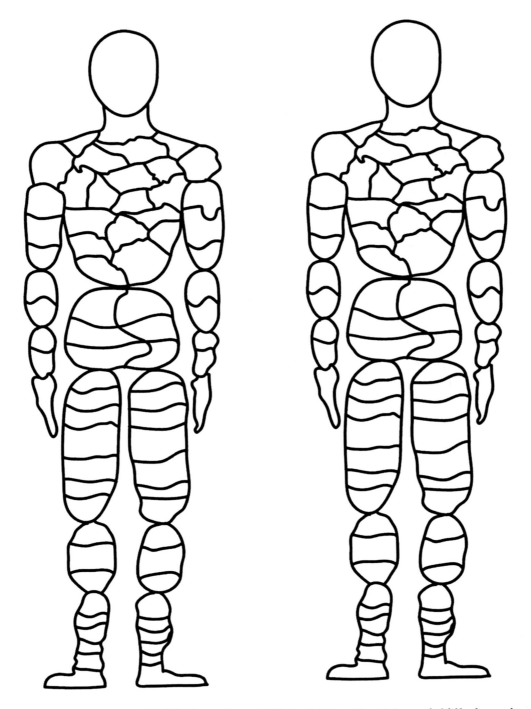

Fill Bubbles #1 with *fulfilled* needs   Fill Bubbles #2 with *unfulfilled* needs

	Never	Rarely	Sometimes	Often	Frequently
1					
2					
3					
4					
5					
6					
7					
8					
9					
10					
11					
12					
13					
14					
15					
16					
17					
18					
19					
20					
21					
22					

Table 3-1: Generic Answer Worksheet

Lightning Source UK Ltd.
Milton Keynes UK
UKOW02f2030280414

230759UK00011B/609/P